Let's find out about...

HEALTHY EATING

Studio Manager: Sara Greasley
Editor: Belinda Weber
Designer: Trudi Webb
Production Controller: Ed Green
Production Manager: Suzy Kelly

ISBN-13: 978-1-84898-090-7 pbk

Copyright © ticktock Entertainment Ltd 2010
First published in Great Britain in 2010 by ticktock Media Ltd,
The Old Sawmill, 103 Goods Station Road, Tunbridge Wells, Kent, TN1 2DP

Printed in China
9 8 7 6 5 4 3 2 1

Picture credits (t=top; b=bottom; c=centre; l=left; r=right; OFC=outside front cover; OBC=outside back cover):
iStock: 10r, 12 both, 22bl. Shutterstock: OFCbl, OFCbr, OFCtr, 1, 4 all, 5 all, 6, 7 both, 8–9 all, 10l, 11, 13 both,
14 both, 15, 16–17 all, 18 both, 19 all, 20, 21 both, 22br, 23 both, OBC. Hayley Terry: OFCtl and throughout.

Every effort has been made to trace copyright holders, and we apologize in advance for any omissions.
We would be pleased to insert the appropriate acknowledgments in any subsequent edition of this publication.

Contents

CUSTOMER SE

Fabulous food

Have you ever wondered why you get hungry? Your body needs healthy food, and there are many reasons for this.

Healthy food keeps your body working properly.

Mixed vegetables

Why do you eat?

You need food to give you energy to play, and do what you want to do. Your body even needs energy to sleep!

What are calories?

Some kinds of food give you lots of energy. The energy in food is measured in units called **calories**. Food that is high in energy has a lot of calories.

How are you feeling?

If you want to stay well, you need to eat healthy food. Eating too much of the wrong kind of food can make you ill.

If you are unwell, eating good food may help you get better.

Talking Point

Why should you try to eat healthy food?

Fresh food is usually better for you as it contains more of the essential **vitamins** and **minerals** you need. Try to eat as much fresh food as you can.

Children need to eat healthy food to grow.

5

Eat your five-a-day

You need to eat five portions of fruit and vegetables a day. A portion is a whole piece of fruit, a serving of one vegetable or a fruit juice drink.

Vitamins and minerals help you to grow.

What are vitamins and minerals?

Vitamins and minerals are nutrients that are found in fruit and vegetables. They help to keep you fit and well.

WORD WIZARD!

nutrient

A nutrient is a natural chemical in food. Nutrients help you to grow and stay healthy

Eating plenty of fruit and vegetables can help to prevent heart disease. It will also help to keep your digestive system healthy.

What is fibre?

Some food is hard to digest. This means it takes a while to pass through your body. **Fibre** is a nutrient that helps **digestion**. It is found in many fruits and leafy vegetables.

Fruit and vegetables contain fibre.

Talking Point

What should you do if you don't like fruit or vegetables?

Try drinking fruit juice – a pure fruit juice drink counts as one portion of fruit. Do keep trying to eat fruit and vegetables. As you get older, you may find that you like them!

Food for life

You need energy to get fit and keep your body healthy. Some high-energy foods help you stay active for longer.

What are carbohydrates?

Carbohydrates are foods that are high in energy. They are very filling, and stop you feeling hungry again for a while.

Playing sport uses up energy, which makes you hungry. You need to eat to get your strength back.

Foods that contain carbohydrates include bread, rice, pasta and potatoes.

What are pulses?

Pulses are seeds that grow inside plant pods, for example beans and lentils. Pulses add **protein** to your **diet**, especially if you don't eat meat.

Pulses

TALKing Point

What types of food give you energy?

Carbohydrates provide most of the energy you need. Your body breaks them down into glucose, a type of sugar that the body can use for energy.

Wholemeal bread

What are whole grains?

Try to include whole grains like wheat, barley and oats in your diet. Whole grains are natural, and are not processed in a factory. They are a good source of fibre, vitamins and protein.

Choose whole grain food, for example eat wholemeal bread instead of white.

9

Do you drink milk?

Dairy foods come from farm animals that produce milk, such as cows and goats. Cheese and yoghurt are made from milk, and are kinds of dairy food.

What's the alternative?

Some people choose not to eat dairy foods, or they can't because they are allergic to them. There are lots of different milk substitutes, including soya milk and rice milk.

Dairy foods contain a nutrient called calcium, which is good for your bones and teeth.

Cow's milk

Soya milk

Some people prefer to drink soya milk. Soya is a vegetable product.

Are eggs dairy food?

Eggs are not a kind of dairy food, but they are not meat either. They are an animal protein, which helps your muscles and bones to grow.

Free-range chickens are farmed in a natural way, and can go outside to find food.

WORD WIZARD!

allergic
If you are allergic to something, you have a sensitive reaction to it

Why are dairy foods good for you?

Dairy foods contain **calcium**, which helps your teeth and bones to grow and stay strong. Children need more calcium than adults because their bodies are still growing.

Eggs

11

Eating meat

Meat is good for you because it contains protein. This nutrient helps you grow, and repairs damage to your body.

Meat can be an important part of a healthy diet.

Steak with vegetables

What kinds of meat are there?

Red meat includes beef and lamb, and white meat includes chicken and pork. Most fast-food meals contain processed meat. This is made from meat, but has other foods added to it.

Do you like meat?

A small amount of meat is good for you, but don't eat too much every day. Many shops sell alternatives to meat, such as soya and tofu.

Many burgers contain meat, but they are also full of fat and salt. Don't eat them every day.

12

What is a vegetarian?

Vegetarians never eat meat. If they are careful about what they do eat, they can still have a **balanced diet**.

Talking Point

What is a vegan?

Vegans are vegetarians who don't eat any animal products. They don't eat eggs or cheese, or drink milk. Many don't wear leather or wool, or eat honey as it's made by animals. They get all their nutrients from vegetable products.

Cows provide lots of our food. Milk, butter, cheese and beef all come from cows.

Do you eat fish?

It is a good idea to eat fish twice a week. One of your fishy meals should include oily fish, such as kippers, salmon and sardines. Oily fish are full of healthy nutrients.

Oily fish contains vitamins that are good for your eyes, skin, hair, bones and teeth.

Salmon

Why choose fish?

Eating fish adds protein to your diet. Fish are also rich in minerals, and are not as fattening as some meats, for example pork and lamb.

Fresh fish

Which fish is best?

The oil in oily fish is called unsaturated **fat**. It contains a nutrient called omega 3, which helps your heart to stay healthy. It also helps different parts of your body to work well, for example your brain.

Eating olly fish is good for your brain, and may help you to concentrate on your work.

Talking Point

Why is fish good for you?

Fish is full of healthy vitamins, minerals and protein. Oily fish contains a healthy kind of fat that is good for your heart and brain.

WORD WIZARD!

unsaturated fat
This kind of fat is liquid at room temperature, and can be good for your heart

15

What are fatty foods?

You don't need much fat in your diet. The two main kinds of fat are saturated and unsaturated fats. Unsaturated fats are better for you than saturated fats.

What shall I eat?

When you can, try to choose foods that are made with unsaturated fats. For example, eat nuts instead of crisps.

Doughnut

Doughnuts contain saturated fat. They should only be eaten as a treat.

Nuts and olive oil are good sources of unsaturated fats.

Talking Point

Why should you try not to eat fatty snacks?

Snacks that are full of saturated fats are bad for your heart. Fatty snacks can make you put on weight. Choose a healthy snack instead, such as a piece of fruit.

Sweet potatoes have more nutrients than ordinary potatoes.

Biscuits, cakes and chocolate contain saturated fats.

Sweet potatoes

Is it fattening?

Fatty foods give you energy, but make you put on weight if you eat too much. Starchy foods, for example sweet potatoes, fruit and vegetables, are also high in energy, but much less fattening.

17

Snack attack

Sugar and salt are often added to food to make it taste nicer, but you don't need lots of sugar and salt in your diet. Too much sugar will rot your teeth, and too much salt is bad for your health.

Many snacks contain salt or sugar.

Salty snacks

Avoid tooth decay

Try not to have too many sugary foods and drinks. Sugar that is left in your mouth turns into a sticky substance called plaque, which can cause **tooth decay**.

Clean your teeth about one hour after you eat sweets.

Does it need salt?

Many **convenience foods** are very salty. You don't need to add extra salt. A salty diet may lead to heart problems.

Oven chips are a type of convenience food.

Talking Point

Why do manufacturers add salt to food?

Adding salt to food is a good way of making it last longer. Throughout history it was used as a way of storing food. It also improves the flavour of some food.

Make a choice

Not all snacks contain added sugar or salt. Next time you are hungry, try eating some fruit, plain popcorn, unsalted peanuts or breadsticks.

Breadsticks

Fruit

Drink up

You need to eat, but you also need to drink in order for your body to work properly. About two-thirds of your body is made up of water!

Try to drink at least one or two litres of water a day. Don't have too many sugary drinks.

It is a good idea to drink water before and after doing something very energetic.

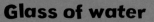

Glass of water

Are you thirsty?

When you **exercise**, you sweat and your body loses water. This makes you thirsty. You also sweat when it is hot, so you should drink more on warm summer days.

Watermelon

Can you eat water?

Fruit contains water, and is good to eat. About half of the water you consume is in the food you eat, and the rest is in drinks.

What is a balanced diet?

You should eat three meals every day, with one or two healthy snacks and lots of water. Remember to eat food from each of the five different food groups for a balanced diet.

This picture shows how much of each food group you should eat. For example, eat lots of fruit and vegetables, but not much fat or sugar.

Bread, cereals and potatoes

Milk, cheese and yoghurt

Fat and sugar

Meat, fish and eggs

Fruit and vegetables

Apple

Have you had enough?

It is important to have the right kind of food, but also the right amount. Eating too much or too little can make you ill.

Hindus believe that cows are holy animals.

Off the menu?

Some people don't eat particular foods for religious reasons. For example, Jewish people do not eat pork, and Hindus do not eat beef. They can still have a healthy diet.

Talking Point

Why is it important to eat a balanced diet?

A balanced diet will give you all the different nutrients you need to stay healthy. Eat lots of different kinds of food, from each of the five main food groups. Don't be a fussy eater!

Are you hungry?

Don't fill up on fatty snacks between meals. Instead, choose high-fibre snacks. They stop you feeling hungry, because they take a long time to digest.

Glossary

Balanced diet: the food you eat that contains all the nutrients you need to be healthy

Calcium: a mineral found in some foods that is good for bones and teeth

Calorie: a unit for measuring the amount of energy produced by food

Carbohydrate: an important source of energy in your diet

Convenience food: ready-made food that is quick to prepare

Dairy food: food that comes from farm animals that can be milked

Diet: the food that you usually eat

Digestion: the way that your body processes the food you eat

Exercise: energetic activity that makes your body strong and healthy

Fat: an element in food that gives you energy, but can make you put on weight. You do need some fats in your diet

Fibre: a substance found in food that helps your digestion

Mineral: nutrients found in food that your body needs to stay healthy

Protein: a substance in food that helps your body grow and keeps it strong

Tooth decay: damage to a tooth caused by sweet food

Vegetarian: someone who does not eat meat, meat products or fish

Vitamin: nutrients found in food that you need to grow and stay healthy

Index